The Dark T[...]

Exploring the Black Death [...]

By *Cindy Wright*

PLAGUE COTTAGE

Mary Hadfield, formerly Cooper, lived
here with her two sons, Edward and
Jonathan, her new husband, Alexander
Hadfield and an employed hand
George Viccars

George Viccars, the first plague victim,
died on 7th September 1665
Edward Cooper, aged 4 died on the
22nd September 1665
Jonathan Cooper, aged 12, died on the
2nd October 1665
Alexander Hadfield died on the
3rd August 1666
Mary alone survived but lost
13 relatives

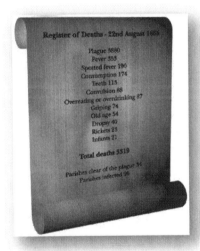

Register of Deaths - 22nd August 1665

Plague 5880
Fever 353
Spotted fever 190
Consumption 174
Teeth 113
Convulsion 88
Overeading or overdrinking 87
Griping 74
Old age 54
Dropsy 40
Rickets 25
Infants 21

Total deaths 5319

Parishes clear of the plague 34
Parishes infected 96

The Dark Traveller

Cindy Wright

Copyright © 2012 by Cindy Wright.

ISBN: 978-1-291-03530-8

To order additional copies of this book, contact:
Email: freedombutterfly7@gmail.com
Website: http://www.cindys-ebooks.webplusshop.com

Also by Cindy Wright

(Available on Amazon Kindle)

Travelling Through the Emerald Isle

The Popular Seaside Places Of The United Kingdom

Worlds of Ice

Part of Your World

Aerobics: A Guide to Keeping Your Heart and Body Healthy

Addition Package

Contents

As people travelled, so too did the plague. Travel between towns and villages in the England of the 1660's were not nearly as easy as it would be today. Back then, it would take days to make a trip that these days would take only a few hours. Viruses and diseases would easily have been spread from one's departure point to one's destination, likely with stops along the way. Inns and public houses could be found in most villages, and were places where many people gathered to feast and drink, in fairly unsanitary conditions, sporting poor hygiene themselves. If one did not have a friend or family member to lodge with along their journey, they would have spent time in these buildings, easily sharing such illnesses as the common cold, or a worse fate, the bubonic plague.

Most often, the travellers were unaware of the miniscule passengers being carried with them, in the form of bacteria or fleas. As little was known in the more educated, and wealthy circles, about how the disease was truly spread, the poorer classes certainly had no clue. Due to the poor hygiene habits of the era, people would wear the same clothing for days at a time, working, sweating, and sleeping in the same outfit. They would not wash their bodies terribly frequently, let alone the clothes they wore. These conditions made clothing a very inviting place for fleas to attach themselves.

The following pages provide a brief description regarding the Great Plague of London in 1665, including symptoms of the disease, prevention methods that were attempted and supposed cures. The toll the plague took on the village of Eyam in Derbyshire is also discussed, as well as what monuments still exist in these locations today that can be visited to document remembrance of the Black Death.

Thought to have originated in Asia, the Black Plague travelled via the Silk Route to cities along the Mediterranean, where it then made its way onto merchant ships bound for European ports. The pestilence had spread to Europe at large by the mid-1300's. London's first known major outbreak of the plague was in 1348, when it killed an estimated 40,000 residents. The city was visited by this disease every 20 to 30 years, killing up to 20% of London's population each time.

By 1665, London's population had grown significantly, and smaller villages were beginning to become part of the greater metropolis. There had been an influx of families moving from the countryside to within the city walls, in an effort to take advantage of London's growing prosperity. Records indicate that the plague outbreak in 1665 again killed at least 20% of London's population; however, the records are somewhat unreliable as the poor were not counted in the beginning, and those in the middle-class frequently denied the death of a member of their household for fear of being house-bound. The city witnessed a staggering amount of death due to plague in a period of approximately 18 months. The estimate of 100,000 victims is likely lower than the true

7

toll. Deaths early on were likely attributed to other causes, and it would not have been until many people were noted to be ill or have died with the same afflictions, that plague would have been suspected.

It took over 150 years for the country's population to recover from the centuries of recurring outbreaks of the Black Death.

The famous 1665 occurrence of the plague was not the worst resurgence in history, but it was the last major outbreak of the disease in England. Thought to have been transported on ships from the Netherlands, where the plague had been occurring intermittently since 1599, the pestilence is suspected to have begun arriving at English ports in the winter months of 1664. Amsterdam alone had seen an estimated 50,000 deaths due to plague between 1663 and 1664.

Recurring trade embargoes had been imposed in association with the Anglo-Dutch Wars over trade and shipping routes. Despite the bans on trade with Amsterdam, the disease may have arrived in bales of cotton, laden with infected fleas, brought by Dutch trading ships during one of many periods of truce between the two emerging nations. Dutch prisoners of war could also have been carrying the disease and spread it to the English soldiers, and they in turn to their families and the population at large.

There is also the possibility the infection was brought by French sailors, two of whom were known to have collapsed suddenly and died in Drury Lane. Witnesses noted unusual, seizure-type behaviour before the sailors died, but attributed their actions to drunkenness. The men were later found to have the same type of lesions on their bodies as those associated with the plague.

The conditions in London were favourable for an outbreak of disease. It had become a thriving metropolis in recent years, and had established trade routes with many parts of the world with the growth of British Colonies in the Americas, Africa and Asia.

A mild winter, that did not kill enough of the rat and vermin populations, was followed by an unusually warm spring and summer, which increased the pest population exponentially. London was heavily populated, filthy and littered, had poor sewage systems, and was rampant with stray dogs and cats. These factors combined to create a feeding frenzy for fleas.

The Bills of Mortality, a list noting the number of deaths and by what cause, were published weekly in each parish. The lists slowly began to indicate the epidemic that was to come.

Ring a Ring O' Roses,

A pocketful of posies,
Atishoo! Atishoo!
We all fall down!

This well-known children's rhyme is often associated with the plague, but its true origins are highly disputed.

The rhyme's association with the Black Death comes from the term 'ring o' roses' being used to describe the red and swollen lesions and sores that would appear on the bodies of those who had become infected.

The posies refer to the herbs and flowers people carried with them in an effort to ward off the disease, mask the smell of death and rot, or disguise the odour of sour smelling breath, which was another symptom of infection.

Sneezing, coughing and seizure, followed by falling down dead, were the final fatal symptoms of the plague.

11

The plague was a horrible disease, both for those who were ill-fated enough to contract it, and for those who had to care for them. How painful it would have been watching the agonizing deterioration of your child or spouse's health, followed by their untimely death. In addition to this, the surviving family member had their own health and potential infection to deal with. The rate of survival, once one became infected, was less than 30%.

At the time, it was not known that the disease was being transmitted via the bite of infected fleas. The curse that was upon London, was seen as divine retribution for the sins that flourish within an increasingly populated and prospering city of the age - drunkenness, debauchery, Godlessness, and filth.

Early diagnosis of one, who had mysteriously fallen ill, was arbitrary speculation at best. There are stories of having citizens breathe on an egg, and should the egg become rotten, the patient was presumed, of course, to be infected. They would subsequently not receive their certificate of good health.

The infection would usually begin with chills and a general feeling of malaise. This would be followed by a high fever, muscle pains, headache, and the most recognizable symptom: swollen lymph glands known as buboes. These sores would be found most often in the armpits, groin and neck areas.

The onset of heavy breathing, seizures, and the vomiting and coughing of blood, was an indication that death was near.

The disease was known as the Black Death, or the Black Plague, because of the blackening of fingertips and toes that occurred when a form of gangrene set in. Sometimes the buboes would become blackened as the blood dried. When burst, the sores would ooze black and green puss.

Symptoms would begin to appear within 5 days of exposure. Death was never far behind, typically occurring within a matter of days after the first symptoms were noted. Although suicide and drowning may have been listed on the Bills of Mortality, many of these instances were cases where a victim had recognized they were infected, and chose not to travel the horrid and painful path to death that was before them.

The plague was easily transmittable with such a large population living in extremely tight quarters. Anyone who could get out of the plague-ridden city did so. Those who could not escape suffered on as best they could.

As the dock areas just outside of London were poor and overcrowded, this is where the plague struck first, though proper records were not kept. The residents of the dockyard tenements were employed to unload the ships in port, bringing them into contact with potentially infected sailors who had travelled from other countries, as well as the perceived source of the plague, the flea-ridden bales of cotton.

The lower classes living in these derelict areas of the city had less value than livestock, in the eyes of the wealthy. In the beginning, the outbreak was even known as The Poore's Plague. It is suspected that hundreds perished in the dock areas before the epidemic reached the parishes just outside the city walls. Many parishioners died before physicians began to recognize the signs of plague, and the the Bills of Mortality incorrectly noted fever or consumption as the cause of death.

The parish of St. Giles-in-the-Fields, is widely believed to have recorded the first deaths attributed to the plague. Though the parish had only 2,000 households, the neighbourhood was hard hit, registering over 3,000 deaths due to plague during the outbreak.

As with many historic records of the times, there are discrepancies. Notations can be found to indicate one Margaret Porteous was the first recorded death due to plague, and that she was buried in Covent Garden, to the south of St. Giles-in-the-Fields, on April 12, 1665. This is, incidentally, the same date many other notations indicate the widow Rebecca Andrews succumbed to the infection, and that hers was the first properly recorded death of the outbreak. Rebecca lived even further east of the two previously noted locations, among 30 other families, in the crowded Cock & Key Alley in the parish of St. Dunstan's. She fostered orphan and lame children who had been left to the streets, and was looking after a boy named Lawrence at the time. When she fell ill, and the physician confirmed she had contracted the plague, Rebecca was shut into her house along with Lawrence. The blacksmith fitted the lock on the door, the windows were boarded from the outside, and neighbours took turns standing guard to ensure no one escaped and infected others in the alley.

The plague soon reached its deathly grip inside the stone walls that surrounded London proper. In June of 1665, the streets were packed with people trying to escape the city. The gates had been closed in an attempt to contain the infection, and only those with a proper certificate of health were permitted to leave. Many forgers made a pretty penny creating counterfeit documents, as the papers quickly became more valuable than gold coins.

By July of 1665, King Charles II, his family and his courtiers, felt it prudent to head to the countryside, and fled the city to avoid contamination. Parliament continued to rule London from a distance, convening at Oxford.

Businesses began closing, as wealthy merchants left the city, leaving many in the lower classes without employment. Anyone with the means to escape did so, including many clergy, apothecaries, and physicians. The Aldermen and city authorities, as well as the Lord Mayor, Sir John Lawrence, stayed behind in an attempt to maintain order within the city walls.

W.J. Gent of London, extensively details the measures to be taken during the time of the plague, from how to clean and purify the air and water, to drawing the poison out of the buboes, in a book dated June of 1665 titled 'A Collection of Seven and Fifty approved receipts good against the Plague : taken out of the five books of that renowned Dr. Don Alexes Secrets, for the benefit of the poorer sort of people of these nations.'. His publication would have been available to doctors and common folk alike.

Fear had flooded the city of London, and caused many families to quickly dispose of their dead in vastly overcrowded pits, creating a new feasting ground for rats and mice, and thus the ever present fleas.

In an attempt to maintain control over the citizens of the city, and their fear, several public health efforts were attempted, many of them by order of the King, Charles II, from his retreat in the countryside.

The Lord Mayor ordered a mass extermination of dogs and cats, as there was speculation that it was these animals that carried the plague. Tens of thousands of animals were noted to have been killed. This culling turned out to be a huge mistake, as the cats in particular would have hunted and killed the rats and other vermin, keeping their population in check.

Fires were kept burning day and night in desperate efforts to cleanse the air. The fuel for these fires often included strongly scented items, such as frankincense, pepper, or hops, which were thought to repel the contagion.

Further use of smoke to purify the air included urging residents to smoke tobacco to ward off infection. This included providing tobacco products to very young children to smoke or even just to chew.

The Gates of London were sealed in an attempt to control the spread of the epidemic to other parts of England. No one was allowed in, and no one was allowed out without a proper certificate of health.

Public meetings, feasts, and gatherings were prohibited. This included worship services, which, if and when they did take place, were conducted outside.

A home where it was known that an inhabitant who was infected with the plague was resided had the doors and windows boarded from the outside, the family trapped inside, and guards stationed to ensure no one escaped. A red cross was then painted on the door with the words 'Lord have mercy upon us'. Anyone in the family who was not initially infected was almost certain to die, living in such a confined area with one who was ill. It was not unheard of for those imprisoned in their own homes to go to great lengths to escape, not the least of which was to bribe, hang, shoot, or stab the watchmen.

Forty days after the recovery, or more likely the death, of the infected person, the boarding could be removed from the home and a white cross painted on the door. The house would then be required to be washed top to bottom with lime. No articles from the home were to be moved to another house for at least 3 more months.

Anyone who tended the sick, the dying, or the dead, was required to carry a coloured staff as to easily be identified and avoided in the crowded streets.

Houses were to be kept clean, and no rotting trash was to be left in the narrow alleyways.

Public houses were not to remain open past 9:00pm, though this regulation was often ignored, and there were not enough lawmen left in the city to enforce such a rule.

Despite the best efforts of the Lord Mayor and Aldermen to contain the plague, most of the stipulations from the King, though set out as laws and punishable if not followed, were ineffective.

A number of Londoners figure prominently in documenting the tragedy of the Great Plague of London in 1665.

One of the more recognized of these figures was a diarist named Samuel Pepys. Samuel was a naval administrator, and had the means to leave the city, as well as the connections required to obtain a certificate of health, but he chose to remain in London, and provided his observations of the plague year in his now famous diary. His accounts are among the best records available to historians on the matter of the suffering of the peoples of London during the plague. He also provides numerous writings of the trials and triumphs of his daily life, as well as his evening escapades, having sent his wife to Woolwich to spare her the hardships that had befallen London.

Samuel did not live in the cramped conditions that many others endured, but in the more wealthy area of Seething Lane in St. Olave. His commentary on what he saw in the streets, and of the tragedy that was playing out before him, provide a vivid description of the events, and sentiments, of the time. Both he and his wife, Elisabeth, survived the outbreak, and subsequently the Great Fire in 1666.

Henry Foe, a saddler, also left diaries, which were likely used by his nephew, Daniel, as a basis for the fictional account 'A Journal of the Plague Year'. The novel was published under the name Daniel Defoe. Daniel was only a child during the plague outbreak, and lived with his family in St. Giles Cripplegate. Although the stories are fictional, they do paint a realistic portrait of London at the time. Luckily, Daniel was never inflicted with the pestilence. His family home, and one other, were the only houses left standing in the parish after the Great Fire. After surviving these tumultuous events, as well as attacks on London by the Dutch, Daniel went on to write such works as Robinson Crusoe.

Others who documented the plague include W.J. Gent, noted previously under the section regarding prevention; John Graunt, whose work 'Natural and Political Observations Made upon the Bills of Mortality' aided in the first proper estimation of the population of London; and William Boghurst, an apothecary, whose writings are discussed later in this book.

The death rate steadily increased as the plague ravaged the city. Some parishes recorded hundreds of deaths, while others recorded none. Few parishes would have been spared entirely, but to shield themselves from house-bounding and other envisioned persecutions, parishes may have opted to deny anyone died from plague that particular week, and noted the death under another cause on the Bill of Mortality. As the warm summer weather fuelled the rotting of waste in the streets and the proliferation of rats and mice, records indicate that by September, deaths in London had skyrocketed to as many as 7,000 per week.

In the autumn of 1665, London was likened to a ghost town. Those living in the rest of England avoided Londoners 'like the Plague', even if the Londoner was known to have a health certificate, as the paperwork could be a forgery. With the gates to the city closed, and a ban on public gatherings, there was no trade, and the economy deteriorated.

People's businesses and livelihoods continued to suffer terribly. Many could not pay their rents due to their loss of employment, and so became part of the raft of homeless, left to beg for food in the streets. In the desolate alleys and avenues, grass started to grow where carts and people previously trod. The squalor and filth, that was already rampant, increased, providing fuel for the spread of the infection.

The Searchers of the Dead were primarily old women, selected for the job as they were reputed to be honest. They were paid to determine the cause of death, and scuttled around after dark seeking out corpses. These women were often bribed not to deduce plague as the cause of death, so as to avoid a home being boarded.

Another sound of the night would have been the so called Death Carts that trolled the streets, with the carriers shouting 'Bring out your dead'. These men, as well as the undertakers and gravediggers, were paid hefty sums to continue their work. It was an early form of 'danger pay', with the knowledge that these professions, having inordinate contact with plague victims, would likely be killed by the disease themselves. The higher wages were meant to leave additional funds for their family after their passing; however, after working with death for days on end, the coins were invariably squandered at the pub.

The smell of rotting waste, the overpowering smell of death, the utter

depravity of the people in the streets, and the incessant tolling of funeral

bells would have made it very difficult to escape the reality unfolding

outside one's front door.

William Boghurst, an apothecary and general practitioner from St. Giles-in-the-Fields, wrote an account of the events of the plague, and his thoughts on cause and treatment titled 'Loimographia'. It is a fantastic work for historians to study, and indicates that Boghurst recognized the cause of the epidemic to be likened to a poison of the blood, and that unusual weather, such as the mild winter and abnormally hot spring and summer, assisted in the plague's rapid spread and persistence. In his work, he also noted occurrences that foretold a coming plague which were of the more superstitious variety, such as children playing at a funeral being ill advised and a bad omen. He gives no small importance to the role of avoiding sin lest the wrath of God be upon you.

Boghurst lists over 50 observed symptoms, and numerous postulations on which types of individuals became infected, and why they were more susceptible to the illness. He also discusses that those who tried hard to avoid the plague, by washing, keeping to themselves, and avoiding corpses and waste, suffered worse when afflicted than those who did not have the means to maintain better hygiene.

Boghurst goes on to criticize the departure of the physicians and apothecaries who left for the countryside in the interest of self-preservation, and who should have stayed in London to administer to the poor and those in need.

In all truth, there was no cure for the Black Death. Many purveyors of remedies surfaced, and they sold their wares under the guise of being doctors, nurses, or apothecaries. They sold pills, ointments, salves, and pomanders, at exorbitant prices. These were desperate times, and they found many a willing buyer.

Some of the remedies being sold were made from recipes that were legitimately thought to be cures and restoratives at the time. Many however were placebos or even poisons. The profits from the sales of their antidotes were frequently used to purchase a forged certificate of health so that they themselves might escape the devastation of London.

Many of the treatments offered by legitimate practitioners involved a complex set of steps using ingredients that the poorer classes would not have had the means of access. One such recipe that was available to the *physicians and apothecaries of the time had been printed in the late 1570's by order of Queen, Elizabeth I:*

"Take of the leaves of Mallows, of Chamomile flowers, of either of them a handful, of Linseed beaten into powder two ounces, boil the Mallow leaves first cut, and the flowers of the Chamomile in fair water standing above a finger's breadth, boil all them together until all the water almost be spent: then put thereunto the Linseed, on Wheat flour half a handful, of swine's grease the skins taken away iii. ounces, of oil of Roses two ounces, stir ... with a stick, and let them all boil together on a soft fire without smoke, until the water is utterly spent, beat them all together in a mortar, until they be well incorporated together, & in feeling smooth, & not rough: then make part thereof hot in a dish set upon a chafing dish of coals, & lay it thick upon a linen cloth applying it to the shore."

The original document was titled 'ORDERS, thought meete by her Maiestie, and her priuie Councell, to be executed throughout the Counties of this Realme, in such Townes, Villages and other places, as are, or may be hereafter infected with the plague, for the stay of further increase of the same. Also, an aduise set downe vpon her Maiesties expresse commaundement, by the best lear-ned in Physicke within this Realme, contayning sundry good rules and easie medicines, without charge to the meaner sort of people, aswell for the preseruation of her good Subiects from the plague before infection, as for the curing and ordring of them after they shall be infected.

Other recommended treatments were contradictory, such as to consume something, or to avoid it, as in the case of alcohol, arsenic, meat, and eggs. Along these lines was the moral battle to either pray for salvation, commit no sins, and avoid the wrath of God, or to commit as many sins as possible so that God would recognize you needed saving and cast his blessing upon you.

Those physicians, apothecaries, and impostors who chose to treat the sick, wore leather masks with glass inserts to shield the eyes, and long pointed noses filled with herbs to ward off the disease and the smell of death. It is a wonder that with such constant contact with infected patients, so many of these doctors did not succumb to the illness themselves.

32

Burn brimstone and allow the smoke to fill the rooms, cleansing and purifying the air.

Burn herbs such as thyme, lavender, sage, rosemary, juniper, and bay leaves, to cleanse the air in your home.

Both the above methods were recommended so as not to allow the disease to spread to other family members.

There were some, however, who believed that immunity to the disease lie in exposure versus avoidance, and could be found inhaling the air from the sewers and latrines.

Suggested remedies to ward off the disease:

Wear a dead toad around your neck. This was believed to be a lucky charm that would keep death away.

Carry flowers or herbs in a posie around your neck or under your nose. If you have the means to purchase strong perfume, douse yourself generously. These strong scents were thought to keep the plague away, and sniffing the flowers and herbs was believed to cleanse any pestilence you may have inhaled.

Do not take payment for goods hand-to-hand, and wash coins with vinegar to decontaminate them. Vinegar was widely available as a cleansing agent, and would possibly have actually killed any pestilence found on the coins.

Pray for the forgiveness of your sins. 1665 was a time when much about disease and pestilence was still unknown. Such a devastating event as the plague would have been seen by the people as being of biblical proportions, and viewed as divine retribution.

Suggested remedies to cure and alleviate symptoms:

Consume copious amounts of 'Plague Water', made from unicorn horn and frog legs, in order to quell fever and body aches. Remedies such as these were available from many a charlatan. No one truly knows what this water contained, and it could possibly have been more poisonous, causing a quicker death, than the plague itself.

Consume hot beverages in order to sweat out the venom of the disease. Sweating a patient was a common practice of physicians in the 1600's. It was believed that causing the patient to sweat profusely released the illness from the body via the skin.

There is a tale of a woman who consumed a large amount of hot bacon fat and recovered from early plague symptoms, though this was likely a great coincidence.

Consume purging pills, which will cause purge, vomiting and bleeding simultaneously. William Boghurst had observed that encouraging the purging of the body hastened the onset of death in most plague patients.

Consume alcoholic beverages, such as brandy, white wine, or juleps instead of beer. The beverage should be warm, not hot nor cold. This was expected to satisfy the extreme thirst that was noted when the patient became feverish. There were additional instructions available as to what types of cordials and tonics were acceptable for consumption by a woman or child.

Prepare a compress of rose, sage, lavender, and bay to relieve headaches. This scent combination is known to actually relieve headaches for some people.

Eat butter or butter with bread. Butter was thought to cure disease and mitigate the effects of poisons.

Pull the tail feathers of a chicken and insert them into the open sores. Many instructions such as this were used in attempts to draw the poison out of wounds. Others involved rubbing the sores with a dead pigeon, or lancing the wound and then covering it with a salve of garlic, butter and onion. It was observed that should the buboes burst on their own, the patient's chance of recovery increased. Unfortunately for the victim, the express bursting of the sores and subsequent rubbing with all varieties of items, more often than not induced additional bacterial infections.

Drink urine. This is an example of the attempt to kill a poison using a poison.

Bleed the victim, using leeches if available. This practice is again one that was common in the 1600's, but opened the patient to potential bacterial infections, or worse yet, they would die from exsanguination.

Consume Red Powder. The ingredients of Red Powder are unknown. This remedy was advertised as being able to sweat out the plague. It may have been a concoction that included crushed peppers, giving the red colour and its consumption making the patient sweat.

Consume a concoction of sorrel, sage and dandelion. This mixture was said to satiate thirst during fever.

Many of these remedies may have in fact helped patients be more comfortable through their illness, but were in general ineffective as cures for the plague.

The winter months of 1665 and early 1666 saw a significant decline in the number of rats, and by consequence fleas, due to the cold weather killing them off. This reduction in vermin also provided some relief from the spread of the pestilence. The number of new cases steadily decreased, and the death rate due to plague dropped considerably.

As the Bills of Mortality continued to report a decline in plague deaths week by week, King Charles II returned to London in February 1666, under the correct presumption that the worst of the epidemic had passed.

In the spring and summer of 1666, the death rate continued to decline, providing additional confirmation that the worst was over. The Black Death had all but petered out when in early September; a fire began in the bakery of one Thomas Farriner. Much of the city was built with kindling in those days: wood, thatch and tar paper. The Great Fire of London raged for 3 days, killing off many rats and burning rubbish that had accumulated in the streets. The blaze was not the victor of the plague, but likely had a hand in dealing the final blow to its riddance.

The population had been decimated, the economy was in shambles, and due to the Great Fire, the city needed significant reconstruction. After the Great Fire, there was an attempt made to suggest the building of wider streets to alleviate congestion. In many places, however, the parishes rebuilt the streets exactly as they were. The need for good hygiene was also recognized, and better sewers and water systems were constructed.

By the time the plague was all but gone from the city, the damage was already done: Merchant ships had already sailed out of London, travelling the trade routes to other European cities. These sailors unknowingly carried the Dark Traveller with them, and spreading the plague to new ports.

In August of 1665, the Black Death arrived in the now famous village of Eyam, located in the heart of the Derbyshire Peak District. Eyam was a small mining town at the time, and its total population in 1665 is widely disputed. Figures for the number of residents living in the village before the plague struck ranges from 350 up to over 800.

Knowledge of the devastation the plague could cause was widespread in England, as they had been visited by the Black Death many times before. Even the smaller towns and villages would have been well aware of the pestilence that was raging in London at the time. The villagers of Eyam did not consider the plague of 1665 to be a great threat to their lives, as the village is located a good distance from the city, and London had closed her gates in an effort to keep the epidemic from spreading north.

George Viccars was a travelling tailor who had set up shop in Eyam for a time. In the 1600's it was common practice for those in the tailoring profession to travel from town to town seeking business. George had ordered some cloth and supplies from London, and luckily, the supplier was able to obtain a certificate of health for his delivery boy, which allowed the boy to leave the city to make the delivery. Travel from London to Eyam would have taken a number of days, depending on the method of travel, and it would not have been an easy road.

It is unclear whether the fabric that was received was new or used. There is speculation that the package contained used clothing, which would have been retailored and sold as being made from the most fashionable cloth of London. There is even the possibility that said clothing came from the belongings of deceased plague victims. High quality fabric was rather expensive in 1665. The repurposing of someone's belongings was not unheard of, particularly when there was no money to be found to pay the debts of the deceased, at which time their things would be taken as payment or sold.

On delivery to the tailor's cottage in Eyam, the cloth was found to be rather damp, so George and his apprentice laid the fabric out by the fire to dry. Unbeknownst to the two men, this action of warming the fabric released an infestation of fleas that had been living on the cloth. These fleas proceeded to seek out food, biting their victims, and transmitting the plague to George and several members of the household. Discovering bites on one's body would not have caused any alarm. Insect bites were common and the itching they caused was just an annoyance.

Within a few days of opening the package, George became ill and had an incredible fever. It was not long before other symptoms of the plague began to manifest themselves, and George died in a most violent fashion, seizing, hallucinating from the fever, and vomiting blood.

His death was closely followed by that of the sons of his land-lady, only days later. Soon after that, the family members of the closest neighbours became ill and died. The Dark Traveller had officially arrived in Eyam.

It was September 1665, and London was at the peak of the epidemic, publishing Bills of Mortality, which recorded over 6,500 deaths per week due to plague. The severity of the outbreak in London, coupled with the death of 10 of Eyam's residents in the month following the passing of George Viccars, would have been enough to cause panic and chaos in the village. This, however, is not how the villagers of Eyam reacted.

Eyam is best known today for the steps the villagers took to prevent the spread of the plague to the surrounding parishes. In 1665, it was not clear to people how the plague was transmitted, other than from close contact between people and their belongings. The citizens of Eyam would have received the same orders from King Charles II as people living in London, dictating measures to be undertaken to limit the spread of infection.

An additional 25 deaths attributed to the disease were recorded by the parish church in Eyam by the end of November 1665. The plague appeared to subside during the winter months, mimicking the events unfolding in London. This was of course due to the rats and fleas dying off during the colder part of the year. Only 28 more deaths were recorded between December 1, 1665 and March 31, 1666. Spring again showed signs the plague may be ending, with a total of 13 deaths in the months of April and May.

For the unfortunate villagers of Eyam, the Dark Traveller was still lurking, and unlike the outbreak in London, the Black Death returned with a vengeance in the summer of 1666. In the month of June, 19 of Eyam's villagers succumbed to the infection.

It was at this time that the Reverend William Mompesson and his predecessor, Thomas Stanley, convinced the villagers of Eyam that drastic measures needed to be taken in order to end the infection and suffering. It was decided that no more burials would occur in the churchyard. Citizens were to bury their dead quickly, at a depth of at least 6 feet below ground, and on their own properties if possible. The depth of the makeshift grave was important, as it was believed that the pestilence could survive and escape a shallower hole.

Although Reverend Mompesson is the one revered for having helped save the north of England from the plague, Reverend Stanley was well known and more popular among the townsfolk. Thomas Stanley had served as rector in Eyam for 16 years prior to be ousted at the time of the restoration of King Charles II, because of his Puritan views. He had remained in Eyam, ministering to those in need, despite having no position. For this reason, it is more likely that it was Reverend Thomas Stanley who was most influential in convincing the villagers not to flee, and directing the course of Eyam's history.

The Reverends had closed the church in June of 1666 as a precaution against gathering a crowd in a confined space. They continued to minister public worship services outside in the fresh air, in an area, which came to be known as the Cucklet Church.

This natural setting was also the site where Emmott Sydall, of Eyam, and her fiancé Rowland Torre, of Stoney Middleton, would meet during the time of quarantine. Emmott had lost most of her family early on, as the Sydall home was located in close proximity to the cottage where George Viccars lived. Worried she would catch the plague and spread the infection to her beloved, she begged Rowland to only meet her in the delph and keep his distance, so as not to contaminate him. Unfortunately, Emmott did succumb to the disease in April 1666. The only way Rowland knew something was not right was that she no longer came to meet him. He was only able to confirm that he would not marry his love once the quarantine had lifted and he entered Eyam in search of Emmott.

The most radical measure the Reverends proposed was to quarantine the village of Eyam so as not to spread plague to the surrounding towns and villages. The villagers of Eyam bravely agreed to this drastic measure, despite knowing this meant certain death for many of them.

As with the closing of the Gates of London, some of the wealthier families fled the village before the cordon of quarantine was established. Aside from this initial exodus, very few are known to have attempted to cross the village boundary once the quarantine was in place. There is a story of a woman who passed the cordon to go shopping at the market in Tideswell. She was forced to flee home, as she was identified by the market merchants as one who lived in Eyam. She was chased away from Tideswell under a barrage of produce.

For those who remained in Eyam, supplies were still needed. The residents from surrounding communities would leave food and medicine at designated locations for the villagers of Eyam to retrieve. Payment by way of coins soaking in vinegar was left behind, the vinegar being used as a means to disinfect the payment. There is some consent that this exchange was done out of compassion for the sacrifice those in Eyam were making, as well as somewhat selfishly: those living in areas outside the village realized that should the people of Eyam begin to starve, they would leave the village in search of food, and in turn bring the plague to other parishes.

July and August of 1666 were a terrible time in the village of Eyam. Entire families were being killed by the devastating disease. In some random cases, all would die but one member, who never became ill at all. There was no one to tend the fields, care for the livestock, or bake the bread. These summer months saw 133 souls registered in the parish church death records. The cause of the pestilence remained a mystery, and its end was nowhere in sight. Yet the villagers did not flee. They felt bound to their commitment to the Reverends, as it was a commitment to the church. God willing, they would make it through this hellish trial.

With the villagers taking care of the burials of their own family members, there was the question of who would bury the last member to die. Marshall Howe, the village sexton, took on this most morbid of tasks. He was noted to be a man of large stature, and he had become sick with the plague early on. He was one of the very few who contracted the disease, but recovered and went on to live a full life. After his recovery, Marshall and many other townsfolk believed he was immune to the pestilence and could not be infected again.

When the last member of a family succumbed to the plague, Marshall would visit the family's home to dispense with the body. He would collect money and belongings from the home of the deceased as payment for his work. It is likely his contact with the dead and the bringing of their possessions into his home that caused the plague to be transmitted to, and kill, his wife and son. It was not until the deaths in his own family

48

that Marshall began to carry out his duties with compassion and reverence.

The autumn months saw a steady decline in the number of plague victims, and the cooler air again began to quell the pestilence. Hope for survival renewed.

In late autumn, over a year after the plague first struck in Eyam, the village reopened to the outside world. The first visitors to arrive expected to find the village deserted, emptied entirely of life. They feared that volunteers from the surrounding towns would be needed to help clear away months of rubbish and death. They were pleasantly surprised to find a good number of Eyam's population to still be alive.

Many of Eyam's current residents can trace their lineage to those who survived the plague, despite the tragedy carrying on for 14 months and killing at least one quarter of the village population. Scientists believe the survivors may have had a gene named Delta 32, which made them immune to the plague, and research has shown the gene is present in the DNA of many of the survivors' descendants to this day.

Although the story of Eyam is tragic, it also shows a great sense of community in the coming together of the villagers for the greater good: sacrificing themselves so as not to spread the infection and death to other villages.

The sacrifice the villagers of Eyam made left its mark in history. The casualties the village suffered are some of the most well documented of the time. The actions of village are credited as the reason the Dark Traveller, the Black Death, was not able to overtake northern England.

The city of London is a tourist attraction unto itself. Many sites related to the Great Plague of 1665 no longer exist due to the destruction of the city by the Great Fire, the reconstruction and expansion of the new city over the top of the old city, and the bombing of London during the war.

The Museum of London's 'War, Plague and Fire (1550's - 1660's)' exhibit is an interesting visit. The gallery contains numerous artifacts and documents of the time, which showcase the turbulence and tragedy of the era.

Northeast of the city centre one can find Walthamstow's Plague Pit, and Vinegar Alley. The graveyard north of the alley was where the bodies of plague victims were dumped in a pit. Vinegar Alley got its name from the extensive use of the material known to ward off disease that was readily available at the time. Vinegar was used to wash and disinfect the alley after the bodies had been dragged through to the pit.

When London's subway system was constructed, it is said that the Picadilly Line had to include a great curve between Knightsbridge and South Kensington Stations in order to avoid a plague pit. Liverpool

Street Station is rumoured to be built on a plague pit as well. Generally, when in London, you just never know upon whom you may be treading.

Numerous churchyards were used as plague pits in 1665. The dead were not buried in coffins, but rather wrapped in cloth and dumped unceremoniously into the pits. The churchyards at St. Brides, St. Dunstan's, St. Botolph Aldgate, and even St. Paul's is known to have had such pits, though in most cases the ground was repurposed after the dead had sufficiently decomposed and the bones removed from the mass graves. The churchyard at St. Giles Cripplegate is rumoured to have over 300 bodies still buried in a pit.

The city blocks around Fleet Street and Fetter Lane were a hub of plague activity. It is in this area that Rebecca Andrews resided, on Cock & Key Alley. Also on Fleet Street, you will find Ye Old Cock Tavern. Though the tavern closed during the plague year, as the owner fled to the country, this was a favourite pub of Samuel Pepys. Many visitors following plague lore stop here to rest and sample the food and beverage. The original tavern opened in 1549, was renamed several times, but has been in the current location since 1887.

Samuel Pepys became such a prominent figure of the time that his bust has been erected outside the Guildhall Gallery, next to the likes of those of William Shakespeare and Sir Christopher Wren.

The tavern where Samuel Pepys stood and witnessed London burning during the Great Fire, The Anchor in Bankside, can also be visited.

At St. Olave Hart Street Churchyard, you can visit the graves of Samuel and his wife Elisabeth.

Though in London there are few specific monuments to the plague other than a few historic plaques at locations around the city, Eyam is in itself a tourist destination for those seeking plague lore.

Mompesson's Well is located just north of the village. This a place where residents from surrounding communities would leave supplies of food and medicine for the villagers of Eyam, in exchange for coins left soaking in vinegar in a stone trough as a means to disinfect the payment.

Another site that witnessed the generosity of villagers living in the areas surrounding Eyam was the Boundary Stone, or Coolstone. Located to the southeast of the village, the stone has had 6 holes drilled into it where the coins and vinegar were placed. The Earl of Devonshire is said to have provided supplies to Eyam using this stone, in a show of support during the plight of the village.

To the east of Eyam are the Riley Graves. Thought to be outside of the plague zone, the Hancock and Talbot families discovered they were in fact not out of harm's way. Elizabeth Hancock buried her husband and 6 children, all of whom died within one week, and never caught the plague herself. The grave markers of the Hancock family can be found on a hillside, surrounded by a stone wall hung with a sign requesting the reverence of visitors to the site.

It is believed that the Hancocks helped bury seven members of the Talbot family, which is how plague arrived at the Hancock home. Elizabeth Hancock is one of only 2 people known to have left Eyam before the quarantine was lifted. With all the death she had witnessed in her own family, she travelled to Sheffield where her only surviving son resided.

With the closing of the St. Lawrence church during the months the plague lasted, the service took place in a natural amphitheatre known as the Cucklet, or Delph, Church. A remembrance service is held here annually, the last Sunday in August, and known as Plague Sunday.

In the churchyard of the Parish Church of St. Lawrence, one can find the tomb of Catherine Mompesson, wife of the famed Reverend. Although the Mompesson children had been sent to the home of relatives in Yorkshire to escape the plague just before the village was quarantined, Catherine chose to remain and provide aid to the sick and dying, with her husband. Perhaps because she already suffered from consumption (tuberculosis), she knew she would eventually become inflicted with the plague and made the decision to help others for as long as she was able. Catherine was the 200th person to be taken by the plague in Eyam, and is one of only a handful of villagers who were buried in consecrated ground at the time. Inside the church, the Plague Register is displayed, noting the names of the deceased and the dates of their deaths.

St. Lawrence Parish Church, Eyam

A stroll around the village will reveal many well preserved stone cottages of the time. Not far from the church are what have become known as the Plague Cottages. Due to the proximity of homes in the village, the plague that begun at the home of George Viccars quickly spread to the families living in the neighbouring cottages. Plaques outside the homes describe various events that took place in these buildings during the plague, and many of the buildings are set up as museums for the benefit of tourists to the area.

The Miner's Arms, the local pub, was established in 1630 and is still in use today. Just outside the pub is the location of a communal burial plot for plague victims. The pub is thought to be the most haunted building in Eyam.

The Eyam Museum contains displays on local history, with special focus highlighting the events surrounding the plague and the measures the villagers took to ensure they would not spread the plague to neighbouring settlements.

Travelling Through the Emerald Isle

A Journey through the Histories of the Provinces of the Republic of Ireland

By Cindy Wright

Take a journey back in time with Travelling through the Emerald Isle. Learn about the histories of the cities that are prominent attractions in Ireland. This book details the histories of various areas and places located through the provinces of Leinster, Connaught, Munster and Ulster, including Galway, Dublin and Roscommon. The stories are perfect for anyone who is thinking of travelling to Ireland or someone who just thirsts for the knowledge of the land.

Aerobics: A Guide to Keeping Your Heart and Body Healthy

By Cindy Wright

If you have ever wondered just how the body works when it comes to exercise, this book is for you. It provides extensive information on the physiological response of the body and the regular workings of the cardiovascular system. It will give you a better idea of how body fat can affect the body, and some great practical ways for helping to eliminate it. This book is great for anybody who is curious about aerobics and beginning their own path to better health.

Worlds of Ice - A Guide to the Life and History of the Arctic and Antarctic

By Cindy Wright

This brief textbook gives in-depth detail of the types of life forms that are commonly discovered in the Arctic Circle and around the continent of Antarctica. It provides rich information about specific animals, both those living on the land and in the icy waters. It is perfect for anyone wishing to expand their knowledge of the fauna in these ecosystems. Written with enough detail to inform those who are new to Arctic studies of the minor subtleties of life in this area, it is a great starting point for those thirsting to know of these worlds. It is a great book, whether you have previous knowledge or not!

Part of Your World - Practical Earth Science Knowledge for the Real World

By Cindy Wright

This brief textbook offers an easy to understand, comprehensive overview of the most important topics related to earth science today. From astronomy to geology, it covers everything you might need to know for real world application. It features up-to-date information on important topics that everyone should understand. Its primary goal is to help students to increase their knowledge, but it's also perfect for those who have no experience in this area. It's a great place to start learning about how nature works!

Printed in Great Britain
by Amazon

31774932R00035